The Client's Guide to Collaborative Divorce

Your Quick and Practical Guide to the Benefits and Procedures of Collaborative Divorce

JOANNE S. NADELL, ESQ.

Copyright © 2015 Joanne S. Nadell, Esq.
Published by Benleigh Company, L.L.C.
Little Silver, New Jersey, United States

All rights reserved. No part of this book may be reproduced, stored, or transmitted by any means—whether auditory, graphic, mechanical, or electronic—without written permission of both publisher and author, except in the case of brief excerpts used in critical articles and reviews. Unauthorized reproduction of any part of this work is illegal and is punishable by law.

This manual is intended to provide readers with a step-by-step guide to participating in a basic collaborative divorce under the general principles of collaborative divorce practice. It is not intended to offer legal advice or render opinions or options to specific individuals who are contemplating divorce or in the process of one. The procedures outlined herein are customarily used by collaborative practitioners in the State of New Jersey, USA. The procedures set out may need to be modified or corrected to comply with the reader's local collaborative practice group's policies, adopted statewide collaborative protocols, and the reader's home state statutes, rules of court, ethics rules and practices. The author and publisher do not make any representations that the information provided herein is for universal use or be considered legal advice and do not assume any liability or responsibility for a reader's inappropriate or negligent use of the contents of this publication.

ISBN: 978-1-4834-3811-5 (sc)
ISBN: 978-1-4834-3810-8 (e)

Library of Congress Control Number: 2015915394

Because of the dynamic nature of the Internet, any web addresses or links contained in this book may have changed since publication and may no longer be valid. The views expressed in this work are solely those of the author and do not necessarily reflect the views of the publisher, and the publisher hereby disclaims any responsibility for them.

Any people depicted in stock imagery provided by Thinkstock are models, and such images are being used for illustrative purposes only.
Certain stock imagery © Thinkstock.

Author photo by Patty D Marchesi.

Lulu Publishing Services rev. date: 9/23/2015

This book is dedicated to my New Jersey collaborative colleagues and wonderful clients who share and help render this remarkable revolution in divorce with me.

A special thank-you and note of appreciation also goes to my colleagues Janis Cooper, M. Madeline Muise, L.C.S.W., and Kathryn S. Lazar, Esq.

Contents

Preface xi

Introduction xiii

1. What Is Collaborative Divorce and How Does It Work? 1

2. Who Participates in a Collaborative Divorce? 5

3. How Long Does This Take and What Does It Cost? 13

Conclusion. 15

Appendix
I. Checklist of Issues for Discussion in Divorce Matters 17
II. Roadmap of the Collaborative Practice Divorce Process:
Neutral Coach Model 20

Preface

My first book, *Roadmap to a Successful Collaborative Divorce: You've Been Trained, Now What?*, published in January 2012, shared my story of discovering the practice of collaborative divorce and chronicled the ups and downs of converting my law practice to one focused primarily on collaborative divorce and mediation. The focus of *Roadmap* was to bring this creative and respectful divorce process to like-minded professionals by providing a tutorial of the process and a library of forms, while encouraging them to embrace the collaborative method.

The Client's Guide to Collaborative Divorce is intended to serve as a basic introduction for clients considering or starting a collaborative divorce. This guide will explain what happens, how it works, who does what, and what the usual costs of a collaborative divorce are.

My law practice is based in New Jersey, so the specific steps and practices I outline herein are used by my practice group, Jersey Shore Collaborative Law Group. They can be broadly applied to most jurisdictions and adapted to conform to any state or regional local customs and rules of practice.

Introduction

This *Client's Guide to Collaborative Divorce* offers an introduction and basic how-to manual for clients who are considering or starting a collaborative divorce. While practitioners around the world may have local rules and systems, I believe that the essential principles and practices of collaborative divorce are universal, so no matter where you live, this guide can be instructional.

My plan is to explain what happens, how it works, who does what, how long it will take, and what the usual costs of a collaborative divorce are. You, the client, can now make the best choice of *how* you get divorced, and I hope that this guide is persuasive and helpful.

Collaborative divorce can be the right fit for most couples facing the end of their marital relationship. By working with a small team of carefully selected professionals, you and your spouse will have all the support and guidance you need to address and ultimately resolve every conflict and issue of your dissolution. Custody, parenting time, support matters, and the accounting for and division of your assets and debts are handled in a confidential, non-adversarial, and efficient manner.

Obviously, nothing in the world, even engaging in a collaborative divorce, will make getting divorced easy. Clients who choose the collaborative divorce process may be just as angry, frustrated, hurt, and confused as anyone else who is going through a divorce.

However, the difference is, the clients make a choice to engage in a divorce process that is centered on protecting their children, fosters client-oriented decision making and lays down the foundation for the clients' separate futures.

I fully appreciate that this may sound like magic to someone on the cusp of a divorce, but I have personally witnessed and participated in this amazing divorce process since 2006. In 2014, nearly half of the cases my office brought to a final judgment of divorce were collaborative cases with signed Participation Agreements.

This new and highly effective way to divorce works for both low- and high-conflict couples and both low- and high net-worth clients. The benefits of engaging in a collaborative divorce are obvious from the first meeting and for years after the divorce is over.

Let's get started.

CHAPTER 1
What Is Collaborative Divorce and How Does It Work?

Collaborative divorce is simply a process of dissolving a marriage in a manner that resolves every issue between the partners without resorting to contested litigation. Many people are not aware that it is absolutely possible to get divorced without the unpleasant drama and high costs of a litigated divorce.

A typical litigated divorce requires voluminous paperwork, includes threatening letters sent back and forth between attorneys, and requires filing expensive interim custody and support applications. It can also require each spouse to spend days in impersonal, dirty and public courtrooms with each other and their respective dueling experts and attorneys.

When you think of divorce, do Hollywood nightmares come into your head? Did your own parents or someone you love suffer through a debilitating litigated divorce? Facing your own divorce, are you terrified of losing your children, your sanity and everything you've worked for and own? Having practiced divorce law for over thirty years, I have witnessed, over and over, the strident panic and pervasive fear my clients feel at the beginning of the divorce process. I know I've found a better way for them.

Every divorce has three main areas of concern that must be negotiated and resolved with great attention to detail:

1. All child-related matters, such as custody, a parenting plan, and child support ;
2. Alimony or spousal support (if any); and
3. The valuation and division of all the shared assets and debts.

What, then, makes a collaborative divorce different and, frankly, so much more humane and efficient than litigation?

In this creative and respectful legal process, each client is represented individually by his or her own collaboratively trained attorney who also, depending on the specific needs of the family, builds a small team of professionals with specialized knowledge and skills to help the clients work things out. Licensed mental-health and financial experts (with much lower hourly rates) are chosen on a case-by-case basis to build a small team that will provide critical guidance on matters and conflicts related to the children and the family's financial situation.

The attorneys and collaboratively trained professionals focus, first and foremost, on the unique concerns and questions that you have about your children and their future. Rather than allowing your children to become collateral damage of a nasty litigated case, we create parenting plans and resolve the numerous financial and emotional issues of parenting without subjecting children to the hostility and turbulence brought on by custody litigation. These team members are known as the "Divorce Coach" and "Child Specialist."

With an emphasis on protecting your children, the collaborative team works constantly to keep the divorce process respectful and manageable. Couples with high conflict especially benefit from the team approach to problem-solving. For some couples, collaboration opens up the paths to communication for the first time in a long time, so that a better understanding of each other and an improved working relationship develops.

Accountants and certified financial planners are engaged as needed to provide an in-depth analysis of your financial situation or to conduct a forensic business evaluation, if needed. "Financials," as they are called on the team, also help craft a fair and equitable division of the family's assets and debt, as well as assisting with determining the appropriate amount of alimony (if any) and child support.

Unlike very public courtroom litigation, a collaborative divorce settlement unfolds privately and confidentially in the lawyers' offices, issue by issue.[1] Meetings, commonly referred to as "four-ways," are attended by the clients and their respective lawyers every few weeks at one of the lawyers' offices. Each meeting has a specific agenda as the team works to identify, address, and ultimately resolve every one of the family's personal and financial issues. Depending on a particular day's agenda, the divorce coach(es) and/or financial neutrals may also attend the meeting.

Four-way meetings start with a discussion of each client's goals, both short- and long-term, for the family, the collaborative process, and their divorce. Each party lists his or her goals and interests; they frequently are pleasantly surprised to learn that their spouse has the same primary goals. Examples of goals are keeping the children safe and well-cared-for, being financially secure after divorce, maintaining a good relationship as co-parents, etc. Identifying their goals aligns the parties and their counsel on their collaborative course.

The most unusual feature of collaborative practice is that the clients and the attorneys actually sign a contract known as a

---

[1] See Appendix, Item I, Checklist of Family Issues

"Participation Agreement," which affirms the clients' promise to collaborate and not go to court to engage in destructive, divisive, and extremely expensive litigation. Experience has proven that, by contracting with each other and their attorneys to avoid court, clients can focus on finding solutions rather than on obstacles to reaching a settlement. Clients can negotiate openly, honestly, and confidentially without the fear of public financial exposure or emotional persecution.

Once a couple has made the commitment to engage in a collaborative divorce, the next step is to assemble their professional team members. Let's take a look now at who participates in the couple's collaborative divorce process.

CHAPTER 2
Who Participates in a Collaborative Divorce?

Two Lawyers

When one or both spouses decide to get divorced, generally one of the first steps they take is to speak to a lawyer. If you find yourself in this position, you have probably delicately polled your family members or friends for a recommendation. It's likely that, in the dead of night or when you are home alone, you have searched the Internet for information on divorce and perhaps looked for an attorney.

I am going to bet that, if you are reading this, you are looking to avoid a horrible divorce experience like someone you know or perhaps your own parents. By considering a collaborative divorce, you are well on your way to engaging in a more creative, respectful, and efficient dissolution process.

A potent contributor to the success of the collaborative divorce process is the engagement of a small team of collaboratively trained professionals who see the divorcing family unit as an entity to be reorganized and strengthened, rather than as two warring factions who have to win their case at all costs. This theme of being helpful and respectful over nasty and divisive operates as the guiding principle in all decisions regarding the children, the clients and the couple's finances.

The first members of the team are the two attorneys, each representing one spouse. To have optimum collaborative representation, each spouse must select an attorney who has completed specific collaborative divorce training and is an active member of their local or state collaborative practice group.

In New Jersey, lawyers must complete a minimum of sixteen hours of basic or introductory collaborative divorce training plus eight hours of mediation training in order to be recognized as qualified to practice collaborative divorce. In addition, it has been my repeated experience that lawyers who participate in practice groups are much more likely to be proficient, have up-to-date training and be committed to the principles of collaborative practice.

Being particular in your choice of counsel will bring you big dividends as your case proceeds. For a national listing of committed collaborative professionals, visit www.CollaborativePractice.com, which is a comprehensive and informative website from the International Academy of Collaborative Professionals.

During your interview, you will feel and hear a whole different attitude from your collaborative lawyer than you'd expect from a typical divorce attorney. We focus on you and your family's future, rather than emphasizing the past and old wounds. During four-ways, we will listen to and treat your spouse and the other lawyer with respect and courtesy. This doesn't mean we sit around and sing "Kumbaya," and there is the normal tension and discomfort this process engenders, but we do our best to act and speak calmly and respectfully.

Don't get worried! Your lawyer is still only *your* advocate and is responsible for protecting your personal and financial interests. Collaborative lawyers work for one client or the other. We simply have a very different approach from our litigation brethren. The lawyers still engage in all the standard tasks of representing a divorcing spouse, such as educating the client about the law, evaluating and implementing custody and parenting plans, engaging in financial discovery and review, and helping clients negotiate a fair, reasonable, and personally tailored divorce settlement.

How does engaging a collaborative lawyer make this divorce process different and less destructive? The difference is that we advocate within the team process and actually work *with* each other and our clients to get the best results. Once the lawyers are retained, the team building starts.

Divorce Coach

The second key member of the team is a divorce coach, who is an experienced licensed clinical social worker, licensed marriage and family therapist, or licensed psychologist. This coach will have been collaboratively trained as well.[2]

Although your divorce coach is a licensed therapist, in the collaborative divorce context, the role of the coach is not to provide traditional therapy to any member of the family. Rather, the coach's focus is on keeping the process moving forward and helping spouses communicate with each other and their children. In high-conflict cases, each client may have his or her own coach.

Divorce coaches assist clients in five major areas within a collaborative divorce:

---

[2] Substantial contributions to this section were provided by my collaborative colleague, M. Madeline Muise, L.C.S.W., who has an extensive family therapy and collaborative practice and is a member of Jersey Shore Collaborative Law Group. Madeline's involvement and efforts as a divorce coach and a team member have helped successfully bring a number of my clients to the other side of their divorce journey.

1. Managing the strong feelings that arise during the divorce process;
2. Developing effective communication skills, including helping clients articulate their needs;
3. Helping clients define their short- and long-term goals for themselves and the family;
4. Developing a child-sensitive and durable parenting plan; and
5. Identifying the skills needed to be a functioning co-parent.

To the divorcing couple, the addition of another member of the team may sound time-consuming and expensive. A common refrain from couples is, "We don't want therapy; we already tried that." However, divorce coaching is not therapy. Rather, the coach uses her or his therapeutic skills and experience to facilitate the process of divorce. Coaching is an efficient and compassionate way to help the couple accomplish the task of transitioning from one nuclear family to a bi-nuclear family.

The collaborative process is sensitive to the issue of cost. Using a coach to move the process along when clients get stuck or mired in difficult feelings is a good use of resources.

In all divorces, the upset and anger between spouses takes its toll on their ability to talk to each other about the big things and the small things of everyday life. Most people getting divorced have experienced difficulties communicating with their spouses for a long time, and coaches help break through those walls. Coaches meet with the couple together and possibly individually, in their own offices, to get to know and understand, from both partners' points of view, the issues and conflicts they are facing as they enter the divorce process.

Couples must make life-changing decisions about whom their

children will live with and where. Detailed parenting schedules including day-to-day parenting, holidays, vacations, and school days all must be negotiated. A myriad of details have to be considered and a comprehensive plan developed for the children's future. If the children are struggling with the divorce or their input is needed or desired, the divorce coach may recommend bringing another mental health professional to the team to act as a child specialist. This person would find and represent the voice of the children only.

Having litigated for so many years, I have sat through more than my share of contentious four-ways between opposing clients and sometimes their lawyers too. The presence of a divorce coach is like a breath of fresh air in the room. Coaches, in their gentle, professional manner, help clients and their lawyers behave better, speak more productively, and stay focused on achieving a resolution. It's actually kind of magical, and my clients have all benefited and handled themselves better with the assistance of their coaches.

The family's parenting plan is the heart of their marital settlement agreement. This plan establishes a schedule that meets the children's developmental needs and provides stability for two-household families. If parenting was a couple's strong point, a parent may not see the need for a formal written plan. I hear parents say, "We'll figure it out as we go along," or, "He (or she) can see the children anytime he wants."

While most parents have these good intentions, life can get in the way of co-parenting. It is wise to write up a clearly defined parenting plan specific to your family. It is a stable reference point as individuals move on with their lives and circumstances change. Children benefit immensely from knowing that their parents have made plans for them.

For couples who are angry and hostile with each other, a

specific written parenting plan is a necessity. Couples often ask the coach, "How can we do this? We never agree on anything!" Or, an individual might remark, "He (or she) is impossible."

Hostility and mistrust are formidable challenges to overcome. Important skills, such as learning to articulate needs, learning to communicate effectively, and learning to manage emotions, all come into play as a couple crafts the parenting plan. This seemingly impossible task for the hostile couple is made possible with the expertise of the coach.

In the beginning of the divorce process, it's a daunting task to think about your future and your children's future. The first challenge for most couples is that of uncoupling. How do you uncouple and still function as co-parents?

In the early stages of divorce, each spouse is generally in a different emotional space. One partner has a foot out the door, and the other partner can't get his or her head around the divorce. In spite of the fact that you might be in two different places, it's important to be present emotionally for the children, establish routines in two separate homes and make the children feel safe, secure, and loved. When you successfully finish your parenting plan, you have laid the foundation for raising resilient children in two households and have taken a tremendous step forward in shaping your children's and your own new life.

The Financial

There are two different roles in a collaborative divorce team that concern financial issues. One is the financial neutral, a member of the collaborative team; the other is a client's financial advisor.

The financial neutral member of the collaborative team must hold a professional license or designation, such as certified public accountant (CPA), certified financial planner (CFP), or other similar license. Known on the team as the "financial," the neutral is collaboratively trained and a specialist in financial matters related to divorce.

Financial advisors, who play a different role from the financial neutral, may be used by the clients individually. The financial advisor role is not neutral. The advisor works exclusively with one spouse or partner. The financial advisor can provide valuable education and financial guidance to one spouse or partner, particularly if one lacks experience dealing with financial matters and making decisions. These financial advisors are not members of the collaborative team; they work outside the process, offering advice, guidance, and some advocacy for their individual client.

As a team member, the financial neutral has several key areas of inquiry and input:

1. Budgets and expenses: Helping clients identify and itemize their joint marital expenses is a good beginning. Once the current marital lifestyle is assessed, the next assignment is for each spouse to make a best-guess estimate of what his or her future expenses with a separate household will be.

   Doing this painstaking analysis of what the family currently spends and calculating how much money the family will need going forward assists clients in preparing their future budgets. This ensures that the parties understand how much money they will need to meet their needs, and their children's needs, after the divorce.

2. Assets and debts: Financials can assist parties with identifying and determining the value of each of their respective assets and debts. Collecting account information, quantifying retirement assets, and conducting a forensic evaluation of a client's business are examples of this service.

Summarizing mortgage debt, credit-card debt, loans to and from family members, car loans, and business loans is also very helpful in organizing the family's finances for the clients and the rest of the team.
3. Alimony or spousal support and child support: After analysis of the budgets, incomes, and goals of the couple, the financial neutral can assist counsel in preparing parameters and proposals for the calculation and amount of spousal support or alimony (if any) and child support.
4. The financial neutral can also offer valuable tax advice regarding the income and other tax consequences of the payment and receipt of alimony and the allocation and distribution of assets, as well as tax ramifications of distributing pre-tax retirement assets and pensions.

Having these matters addressed and studied by the financial neutral adds tremendous depth to the analysis provided to the clients and helps generate informed options for going forward.

CHAPTER 3
How Long Does This Take and What Does It Cost?

A key advantage of collaborative divorce is that the couple or team can control how quickly or slowly the divorce process goes. Litigated cases are time-managed and controlled by anonymous bureaucrats who impose mandatory court appearances and multiple required court filings upon clients.

The collaborative process more appropriately avoids that waste and has flexibility built into it so the team can help the family move ahead at its own pace. Some cases are resolved in a few months; others, interrupted by illness or a job loss, can be discontinued for a period of time, if necessary or preferred by the clients.

Obviously, some cases are more complex than others, so the amount of time and money required to achieve resolution varies. In cases where there are tough communication issues, parenting challenges, or a family business that needs to be evaluated, more time and expense are required.

Collaborative divorce is generally less expensive than traditional litigation, in large part because lengthy and unproductive court appearances are eliminated. The complaint for divorce and streamlined court proceedings do not even start until after the case is settled with a signed marital settlement agreement. If you ask anyone who had a litigated divorce how much time they wasted waiting around with their lawyers at the courthouse, you will understand these savings right away.

Additional savings are incurred when parties collaborate instead of getting two dueling experts on any issue. Clients, with their attorneys' guidance, select a joint expert and hire only one, thus saving thousands, maybe tens of thousands, of dollars. Nor do the lawyers engage in the petty, costly and counterproductive letter-writing campaigns that litigation generates.

Finally, specialized counselors and financial professionals, working at significantly lower hourly rates than the combined price of two lawyers per hour, address the clients' emotional and financial issues in confidence and with greater efficiency helping cases resolve sooner.

Developing a parenting plan with someone who has experience in family transitions and children's developmental issues, for example, is far more effective and less expensive than using two attorneys to accomplish this task.

While it is impossible to predict the length and outcome of every case, the cost and speed of a collaborative case beats the same case in litigation every time.

Conclusion

I hope that this concise description of the benefits and procedures of a collaborative divorce has been helpful to you.

This modern and respectful process offers spouses and partners a method of marital dissolution that makes every effort to preserve the best of their family and help each member move into a new future.

Thank you for taking the time to learn more about the collaborative divorce process. I hope that you will recommend it to any family and friends who may be in need of their own collaborative team in the future.

Joanne S. Nadell, Esq.

Appendix

I. Checklist of Issues for Discussion in Divorce Matters

1. Review status of the pre-nuptial agreement, if one exists.
2. Review goals for future.
3. Children:
   a. Joint vs. sole custody; establishing primary and alternate residences
   b. Review special needs and/or special circumstances related to child(ren)
   c. Parenting time schedule: Regular time, summer/school year, holidays, and vacations;
   d. Other important topics include: Children's transportation; right of first refusal; taking children to activities; significant others, including when they will meet children, notice to other parent first, not being called "Mom" or "Dad"; mutual agreement not to demean or malign other parent; cell phone and social media guidelines; access to online photo sharing site; custody of family pets.
4. Describe employment status/educational background of the parties.
5. Alimony: Prepare family budget and case information statements for each party. Is alimony appropriate? How much? For how long?

6. Review health and dental insurance and uncovered medical expenses for the parties, including the children.
7. Child support: Determine amount per guidelines or appropriate modification of these guidelines; identify triggering events for review of child support amount; discuss and implement direct pay vs. probation dept. or wage garnishment.
8. Document and allocate actual or anticipated college or vocational educational expenses.
9. Emancipation of children.
10. Discuss life insurance, disability insurance, auto insurance, and estate planning post-divorce.
11. Identify, value, and equitably distribute assets, including:
    a. Marital home, vacation home or other real property
    b. Mutual funds, IRA, 401k, pensions
    c. Bank accounts—checking, savings, mutual funds
    d. Vehicles, including automobiles, boat, recreational equipment
    e. Household furnishings and all other personal property
    f. Business(s) or professional practice(s)
    g. Intellectual property, patents, copyrights, etc.
    h. Assets held in or by trust(s) or other fiduciary
    i. Frequent flyer miles or reward points
12. Identify, value and equitably distribute debts and liabilities, including:
    a. Mortgage(s), equity line(s)
    b. Credit cards
    c. Automobiles, boats, or other vehicles
    d. Loans—business, personal, family members
    e. Outstanding line(s) of credit, promissory notes, other
13. Resolve tax issues: filing, apportioning, paying, dependency exemption(s).

14. Obtain referrals to consultants or other professionals, if desired, as needed.
15. Determine responsibility for payment of counsel, coach and expert fees and costs.
16. Other matters particular to present case.

II. Roadmap of the Collaborative Practice Divorce Process: Neutral Coach Model[3]

Both of you want to be treated fairly. "Fair" is a very subjective idea, however, careful preparation and good communication can facilitate and perhaps shorten the process and help us achieve an outcome that is satisfactory to both parties. We have developed the Roadmap to assist you in understanding the process and where you are at any given time.

The precise course of your particular case will vary depending upon several factors, including your individual needs, the complexity of the finances, whether you have children, and if so, the needs of your children.

Warnings:

1. Failure to do your assignments in a timely way will cost additional time and money.
2. Deviating from the Roadmap may cost additional time and money.
3. Failure to use the coach to assist you in managing your emotions will cost additional time and money.

---

[3] Reprinted with permission from Kathryn S. Lazar, Esq., Hudson Valley Collaborative Divorce Association, Hopewell Junction, New York.

Stage 1: Signing on to the Process and Assembling the Team

____ 1.1 Clients meet and hire attorneys.

____ 1.2 Attorneys confer regarding assembling the team, recommend a coach.

____ 1.3 Clients meet with coach, individually and/or jointly, and affirm selection or another coach is selected.

____ 1.4 First five-way meeting at which:

    ____ Participation agreement and release signed;

    ____ Roadmap reviewed;

    ____ Valuation date discussion;

    ____ Cost of collaborative and discussion of how it will be paid;

    ____ Schedule first financial meeting;

    ____ Schedule financial six-way and other appropriate meetings;

    ____ Set up any temporary children/cash flow arrangements.

____ 1.5 Clients meet coach individually and jointly as necessary.

____ 1.6 Clients meet with financial specialist and begin financial information assembly.

____ 1.7 Professionals conference call to assess case and develop overall timing of the case.

Stage 2: Communicating and Gathering Information Regarding Children and Finances

A better outcome is reached after you completely understand your financial situation and the best way to help your children. This stage involves the exchange of all necessary information and creates a good foundation for decision-making.

Children and Communications

___ 2.1 Coach meets with both of you individually and together. Jointly, you determine whether to use a child specialist or have the coach handle this work. Child specialist selected, if indicated, and meets with parents.
___ 2.2 Coach has regular check-in with you and meets with you as needed to stay centered and develop a sense of priorities.
___ 2.3 Coach three-ways, as indicated, to develop parenting plan and facilitate communication. These will be ongoing sessions throughout the process.
___ 2.4 Child specialist meets with your children.

Finances

___ 2a.1 You jointly provide all necessary financial information.
___ 2a.2 You jointly have two or three meetings with financial specialist.
___ 2a.3 Financial six-way: attorneys, clients, coach, and financial specialist meet for presentation of financial picture and determination of what additional appraisal or assessment work is necessary.

___ 2a.4 Additional appraisals or assessment work undertaken and completed; assemble all financial information for a complete financial picture.
___ 2a.5 Second financial six-way, if needed.
___ 2a.6 Professional conference call to decide who should be present at which meetings during Stage 3 and discuss any issues that have developed.

Stage 3: Identifying Interests and Concerns

Both of you want an outcome that meets your most important concerns; in this stage, we take the time to explore your values, your concerns, and your priorities, so that we will be better able to find a mutually acceptable resolution. Instead of getting locked into positions, we need to develop possibilities to help us find the common ground to reach resolution.

____ 3.1 Three-way preparation: You will meet in a three-way with your attorney and the coach to identify your interests and priorities.

____ 3.2 Interest meeting: You will meet in a six-way with attorneys, coach, and financial specialist to discuss and understand each other's individual interests and priorities.

____ 3.3 Brainstorming session: Group brainstorming regarding possible solutions. If possible, develop a "frame" as to what an ideal solution would have to do to achieve both parties' highest priorities.

____ 3.4 Development of alternatives: You meet separately and/or together with appropriate professional team members to review the possible solutions that were developed during brainstorming, to develop options for consideration, and to review implications of different possibilities.

____ 3.5 Child-needs feedback: You meet jointly in a four-way meeting with the child specialist and the coach for feedback from the child specialist.

____ 3.6 Professionals conference call to discuss financial and parenting decision making process, including who should be present and responsible for leading each effort.

Stage 4: Making Decisions

Having done all our homework well, we are now ready to reach conclusions that meet the needs of both of you (and your children). To do this, we need to have an orderly exchange of ideas and proposals, and continue the conversation until we find a result that both of you can accept.

____ 4.1 Financial meetings: You meet jointly in a three, four, five, or six-way meeting with attorneys and other professionals, as appropriate and necessary to present several financial packages, identifying the interests served for each person by each of the possible solutions.

____ 4.2 Settlement meetings: You have settlement meetings as needed with professionals to come to a conclusion regarding the financial plan.

____ 4.3 Parenting plan meeting: You meet with the coach (or as otherwise arranged) to develop the parenting plan.

____ 4.4 Finalize issues: You meet jointly with the lawyers to finalize any open issues and take any steps necessary for implementing the agreement (for example, arrange for refinancing or marketing the house, discuss stock transfers, decide how you are going to do the pension transfers, if necessary, etc., as applicable). You may also agree on follow-up with coach/child specialist regarding the children in the future.

____ 4.5 Professional conference call: Inform all team members of outcome and identify recommendations for couple for future. Team debriefing.

Stage 5: Finalizing and Implementing the Plan

To complete the process, decisions may need to be made about timing and the implementation of the agreement. In order to complete our work, appropriate documents need to be signed by both parties.

___ 5.1 You jointly agree which attorney will draw up the agreement and whether to divorce immediately or wait; paperwork is drawn up by attorneys.

___ 5.2 You jointly meet with the attorneys to revise and sign property settlement/separation agreement and any ancillary paperwork (deed, titles, etc.) and discuss any recommendations from the team. All professionals should be paid in full before the signing occurs.

___ 5.3 Divorce paperwork and pension paperwork completed.

About the Author

Joanne S. Nadell is a collaborative divorce attorney, mediator, author, speaker, and educator with more than thirty years of experience in handling family matters in private practice near the Jersey Shore. Ms. Nadell is past president and board member of her local collaborative practice group and a long-time member of the International Academy of Collaborative Professionals.

Visit AtlanticDivorceMediation.com to learn more about Ms. Nadell's practice and to read her blogs about life and articles in ardent support of the many benefits clients will receive by engaging in a collaborative divorce rather than divisive and wasteful litigation.

Also see by Joanne S. Nadell, Esq., available on Ms. Nadell's website and Amazon.com, *Roadmap to a Successful Collaborative Divorce. You've Been Trained, now what?*

"Thank you for sending me a copy of your Roadmap. I have found it to be a very thorough and helpful resource to help attorneys guide their clients through the Collaborative Process."
—Ron Ousky, Esq. 2012

"What I like and found most useful about your book was the 'how-to' approach, and the clear, sequential format was easy to follow. Theory is great! — but we need THE MANUAL too! It was easy to read, easy to put into practice, and then, easy to remember and integrate."
—Maura Sullivan, Esq. 2014

COMING FALL 2015
YourDivorceBridge.com

Notes

Notes

Notes

Notes

Notes

Notes